Mind travels and Beyond

Anusha Rashmi

BookLeaf Publishing

India | USA | UK

Presentation by *BookLeaf Publishing*

Web: www.bookleafpub.com

E-mail: info@bookleafpub.com

ISBN: 9789363319066

First edition 2024

I would like to dedicate this book to my daughter Brahmi Hegde, for it is she from whom I get immense love.

ACKNOWLEDGEMENT

I would like to express my sincere gratitude to BookLeaf publishers for the writers' challenge that provided me a platform to put up some of my poems for publishing. I would like to express my sincere thanks to my family, friends and everyone I have come across as the poems are an expression of my life experiences.

PREFACE

In a world filled with chaos and confusion, the poems within provide a reality check. The poems try to encompass many real-life situations an individual would pass through during various phases of life. With a blend of facts, humor and thought-provoking poems, this book gives a glimpse into the actual world.

The Twinkling Star

Oh dear twinkling star
Why were we told to wonder what you are?
Because though you are long past gone,
Your shine has been reaching us from so many
lightyears away.

I now know why they taught us all wrong
By calling you little
Because you are in fact a superstar!

Hence
Oh shining star!
Your light reaches us through the darkness,
Because you are away from the worldly
darkness,
And you are a superstar
Because though long gone, you are yet there for
us in this ground.

So
Oh twinkling superstar
How I wonder you are what you are
Up above this world
You shine up so high in the sky

Oh twinkling superstar,
How I wonder you are what you are,
For I would like to be just like you,
Be there and yet not be there

Twinkle twinkle oh superstar
How I wonder you are what you are.

#RashAnu

The Wonderful Surprise

As I stood waiting by the street one late night,
I had no clue that a day would come when I
would be standing alone through the darkness
that surrounded me
And yet not fearing one bit.

Surrounded by cars of big brands and small
As my car lay neatly jam-packed in the midst
I wondered how to get my car out
As there lay no inch small or big
For me to maneuver outside into mainstreet.

As happy as I was to get a parking lot in the
broad daylight
I had no clue, I would have to wait into the dark
hours of the night to just get out!
But then there I lay standing and waiting
For at least one car to move.

Any other day it would not have been easy
But this day was different
Hearing the prayers of hundreds inside a hall,
half a kilometer away
I too prayed along
When the time came to drive away nearing
midnight
I was wondering if I would have felt brave
enough on any other day
To keep waiting by the street all alone until
midnight.

#RashAnu

It is OK

When the light shines bright,
Put on your shades.

When it pours down,
Open your umbrella

It is OK to shield yourself
Because only you know what is best for you.

It is only when you brace yourself
You are ready to face what lies head-on.

#RashAnu

Embrace Life

In the realm of today's world
The mind seems to wonder
Why wander when you now know what your
goal is?
Why wander when you have come to know of
your true self?
Why get constrained in the clutches,
The very same that once gave up on you.
When you can hear your inner self talking now
Free yourself, embrace life, explore more
No matter who thinks what of you,
You know yourself better than any.

#RashAnu

That Voice inside you

When you start understanding Life,
You start getting wiser with time,
Your instincts guide you right,
As the wise voice inside you has now woken up.

You shall be played like a football around,
However, knowing all this, you can still get
around,
Because at the end of the day, it is your rules,
your passion, your principles that matter,
Because these come from within you.
Learn to listen to that voice,
Because that inner voice never betrays you.

#RashAnu

A note to keep

With its enormous combinations of ups and
downs
There is no better teacher than life alone.

We are after all a minuscule in this entire
universe
From experience, we learn and move on

Behold the truth that nobody can bind you
Unless you let the bindings bind you
Behold the truth that you are a free bird
Unless you let yourself be caged
Behold the truth that you have the power to do
what is right
Unless you do what others want of you.

Behold the truth the power to let go is with you,
You need to know when to stay, when to stand
up and when to step down.

#RashAnu

My shining star

Unwell and Down
With head reeling around
Coughing aloud and fever running high
Alas! you feel pretty let down.

But my young one knows a way
To bring a smile on her mamma's face
By giving me her handmade card on Women's
Day.

Her creative spirit is what I love about her,
She goes after me would be an understatement,
As she keeps the bar rolling higher for me,
For it is she who made me a strong woman
Since the time she was born

Her selfless love is what keeps me going
For an observant child, she has become
To understand her mother like no other.

#RashAnu

Time to say Bye to the new normals

Yes, it is time to say bye to the new normals,
Time to say bye to taking work home,
Time to say bye to work meetings at home,
It is time to be at home and feel at home,
It is time to get back to normal,
For if we do not do it now,
The new normal shall become the normal,
And pave the way for many disasters to come.

It is high time to say goodbye to the new normal.

#RashAnu

Be Hassle Free

No worries to endure,
As I bury them immediately,
They get composted
And lo behold!
A composted buried material,
Is very good manure
And good manure provides good nourishment.

When things do not go your way,
Why take the hassle of taking it the wrong way?
Instead, reroute it the right way.

#RashAnu

Mysteries of Life

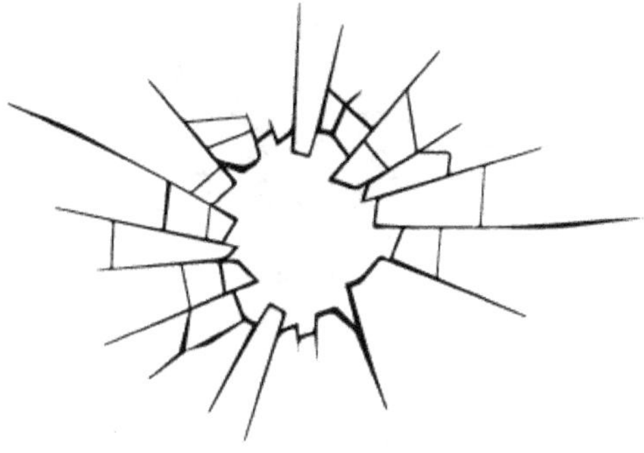

When Life itself is a mystery,
One should not be surprised at what you
encounter,
Life can baffle you, can give you a hell of a ride
Life trains you for the onslaughts, empowers
you with a lot of goodness,
It is you who decides how to flow through it.

Remember the jargon "Change is the only
constant?"
Well, we also must know that we need to be the
change too,
The path of change is ultimately decided by you.

The key to success in every story out there is
accepting change and being the change itself.

#RashAnu

The Kingfisher

The range of colors in a Kingfisher,
So small yet so beautiful,
Nature's creation around keeps reminding us,
That it is the small things we learn to appreciate
that matters.

Highly territorial, the Kingfishers courtship and
then
The kinship with its mate,
Nature's creation around keeps reminding us,
It is partnership that counts.

The Kingfisher strikes hard for its prey with
clarity underwater
Nature's creation around keeps reminding us

That it is not mighty strength but timing that
counts.

15

#RashAnu

The Knee Hammer

There was a hammer once with a tall professor,
Lying in his apron pocket,
It elicited many knee jerks,
And the man's name itself caused many jerks!
For the people around him were very scared
Both of him and the hammer.

He was a dominating character,
That would cause many of us to flee from sight,
Then as students and interns though.
But those were the days when he was our
teacher.

Those scary days have turned into memories,
And we let the hammer memories remain with
us now,
For laughter and glee, not to flee.

#RashAnu

Time to reflect

What are we waiting for to
Start afresh? To do some good?
To hold someone's hand? To help some needy?
Are we waiting for a calling?
Or are we going to reach within us and call out
ourselves?

If our forefathers had waited for the new year's
eve to start afresh,
We would never be living free of domination to
this day.

If our forefathers had lived only for themselves
and not for the country's freedom,
Then what is awaiting the global downfall is
what we would be reaping now.

So, let us think over and start now,
Think not just about ourselves and our families

Think not just about other humans but other
beings on this planet,
For the planet will actually thrive if there are
going to be no humans.

The point however is how conscious of this are
we?

It is time to reflect and think on whether we
need to actually start thinking like evolved
beings or,
Face the consequences soon
And thus go back to Darwin's theory of
evolution.

#RashAnu

Dancing to the music

Dancing enhances the joy within you,
It helps you unleash that child within you,
It helps bring out the inner sculptor within you,
Dancing lets you feel alive in a different way.

It gives way to ways of getting others involved
in your happiness as well,
It just takes a tap or two and then you have so
many tapping alongside you.

Oh, the joy of dancing!

#RashAnu

Self Motivation

Though the heart is loaded,
I have come to peace with my inner self,
That voices out time and again,
That it isn't over for you yet,
Keep going and the purpose will find you,
The one you have been waiting for,
To feel liberated and one with the Supreme

I am thankful that my spiritual self,
Always and always comes to my rescue,
And always provides me the solace and the
solution.

#RashAnu

The Cat life hacks

What a cat can teach you...

One: Attachment with Detachment
A cat shows us to carry out our responsibilities
and then to let go once done
Have no expectations from your children.

Two: Know how to be fierce when required
A cat lets everyone around know that he/she can
be played around
But when things turn uncomfortable he/she can
shoo you off with just the right amount and tone
of meow.

Three: Leave when it is time to
A cat pushes off its own children to start their
own journey,

As it knows that to grow further one needs to go
out of the comfort zone.

Last but not the least
A cat teaches that one needs to take time out for
yourself, groom well, love yourself, work on
your skills, stay active and be flexible
and

There is always some time to just be lazy.

#RashAnu

Advancement or derailment

From enjoying the life bestowed on us,
Evolution, transition or advancements
Seem to have left one thinking,
Just live life or do we have to love life and love
living?

Though the answers have been there from
ancient scriptures,
Even before evolution, transition or
advancements,
It seems to have left one wondering,
What exactly are they doing in life?

The answers appear very clear,
Though everyone seems to be wondering,

One is bothered more about another's growth.

It is time to think about self-growth.

#RashAnu

The Doctor clan

From being frightened of dead bodies, blood and
so on,
To now dealing with all with ease,

From looking at those cells under the
microscope,
To looking at the larger variations and
dimensions through our very own eyes now,

From running, hopping and sneaking into
classes,
From dining and partying and pooling in from
our little pockets then,
To paying the larger bills now

From a heterogenous mixture of people who
came to college,

To graduating into a homogenous tribe called
doctors,
It has been a life-changing experience for each
and every one of us.

#RashAnu

Oh Doc, Please take care.

Be humble, patient, kind and gentle,
But also be stable, as your Vitals are also
essential,
For in every wake of storm, you need to be
calm,
Even when cold and clammy, you need to be
warm.

A profession chosen to be of help to others
Be it any oath on this planet,
We are bound by one common law of nature,
To be there for each other, to walk the right path.

To be there for ourselves, to do good for others
To do what you love and to love what you do
With boundless passion and commitment

And for all this to happen
Oh Doc, you need to take care too.

#RashAnu

Feel the Vibes

Just like

A stare can provoke you,
While a glance can bring a smile on you,

A word said in an empathetic tone can tune you
up,
While a word in a commanding tone can set you
up,

While judgements can shut you up,
But a gentle advice can open you up,

Similarly,

There are vibes around you
That you cannot touch but you can feel
It is all there in and around you,
Just feel it, embrace it and live and love your
life.

#RashAnu

Independence day

Living and breathing independence
With newer generations living it,

Let us be thankful to those wonderful souls,
For all those who laid down their lives,
For us to reap the fruits of freedom.

On whose sacrifices we now walk with glee,

Let the country awake
Not just watch the parade

Let us learn from our forefathers,
To walk together, to think for one another, to
fight for the other.

Bound to each other with this motherland,
For it is she who keeps us together,

Let the country awake not just on one
Independence Day
But let it be on every other day.

\#RashAnu

www.ingramcontent.com/pod-product-compliance
Lightning Source LLC
LaVergne TN
LVHW010938200726
843509LV00013B/2243